MAMA SAID

MAMA SAID

A collection of proverbs with an African-American perspective

Bennie Newroth

Library of Congress Control Number: 2007900694
ISBN: Hardcover   978-1-4257-5140-1
               Softcover   978-1-4257-5112-8

To order additional copies of this book, contact:
Xlibris Corporation
1-888-795-4274
www.Xlibris.com
Orders@Xlibris.com
35632

CONTENTS

This book is dedicated in honor of

Carlo Butler Newroth

Jennifer Kristen Ogletree

John Quinn Newroth

Andrew Jalon Ogletree

Ashlee McKayla Ogletree

And

In memory of

Eva Lou Butler

Margaret Bodye

Eleanor Butler Hauser

Lavonia Pitts Butler

ACKNOWLEDGEMENTS

Mama Said … is an effort to record, for future generations, the words of wisdom from our ancestors. It is not intended to be a scholarly thesis. Rather, it is a fond remembrance of the teachings of our mothers. It is a realization that we are our mother's children and that the same advice we thought we had heard enough of, we are now giving to our children. In doing so, we are, perhaps unwittingly, passing our culture down to another generation.

All the words of wisdom included in this book were not compiled solely from my own personal experiences. Some are from friends and relatives who readily shared their mothers' pearls of wisdom. Most certainly, readers will recognize some of these in some form from their childhood.

It goes without saying that a great many of these adages did not originate with our foremothers. In fact, readers may well discern traces of Shakespeare, of Emerson, of Thoreau, of Ben Franklin, of Jesus, or of any number of historical and present-day voices. However, what I have attempted to present here are our mothers' and foremothers' homespun versions of those truths. Indeed, it is therein that we see their beauty.

A special thanks to the village women: Altheia Butler, Margie Butler, and Arline Kitchen for constant encouragement. To John Butler, my Mr. Mom, for guidance and support. Thank you to some special teachers: Lyda Hannan, Willie Mae Alexander, Marguerite Watt, Alma Bass, and John Washington who taught not only the academic subjects but taught about life and living. Thanks to Bob Hydrick and Morten Harris for sharing words of wisdom. Thanks to Clayton Henry, English teacher extra-ordinare. To Dr. Oscar Pendleton, a special thank you for his support and encouragement.

"Next to God we are in indebted to women,
first for life itself,
and then for making it worth living."
Mary McLeod Bethune

"Who ran to help me when I fell,
and would some pretty story tell,
or kiss the place to make it well…my mother."
Ann Taylor

"All good traits and learning come from the mother's side."
Zora Neale Hurston

INTRODUCTION

Life is a cycle of endless challenges and changes. Things which were true yesterday are not necessarily so today. Nevertheless, we strive to make sense of our world. And as we struggle to prepare ourselves for this millennium, we question things that are going on around us. Indeed, some of us are unsure of ourselves in our relationships with our mates, with our children, with our parents and with our peers. We live in a constant state of flux. Consequently, we are spending an enormous amount of time worrying. We are buying "how to" relationship books in record numbers. We watch television hoping for a program that will give us answers. We are looking for a guide for living. We search as if there is some type of magical recipe. For most of us, the answers to many of our problems are within us. They are housed in the memories of what our mamas said.

Theirs were the voices of wisdom. Our mothers gave us words of wisdom that had been passed down from their mamas and other women of the village. Such wisdom had a special energy: it affirmed the truth. In many instances, this wisdom was deeply rooted in the African-American culture and in the Bible.

Without an advanced degree, oftentimes without any degree or formal education; without the label of expert, Mama had the answers. With a shake of the head, a hand on the hip, a finger pointing or loving arms embracing, Mama taught us the ways of the world and gave us a code of living. Her wisdom did not require big words or dissertations. Quite the contrary, all that was required was common sense and plain words. Mama used proverbs to express in a few words universal truths and undeniable wisdom. This wisdom has never gone out of style. It is as relevant today as it was when we were children and our mothers were young women.

As we struggle to grow as individuals, to find the right words to say to our children, to make sense of our world; we must return to the source. We must go within and listen to the quiet voices of our mothers and remember what our mamas said.

CHARACTER

Eleanor Butler Hauser

CHARACTER

Eleanor Butler Hauser

A good name is rather to be chosen than great riches,
and loving favour rather than silver and gold.
Proverb 22:1

Birds of a feather flock together.
A hard head makes a soft behind.
Wear you problems like a loose garment.
You are known by the company you keep.
One does not become great by claiming greatness.
Only the strong survive.
Smooth seas don't make good sailors.
Empty wagons make a lot of noise.
You can't judge a book by the cover.
Your character shows when no one is looking.
Sticks and stone may break your bones but talk can't hurt you.
Courage is doing what you are afraid to do.
Walk to the tune of your own song.
The company you keep will determine the troubles you will meet.
Every flower blooms in its own season.
One rotten apple spoils the barrel.
If it walks like a duck and quacks like a duck, it must be a duck.
A hit dog will holler.
Pretty is as pretty does.
A tiger doesn't change its stripes.
Don't scratch you head 'less it itch.
Don't dance unless you hear the music.
Either you is or you ain't; either you do or you don't; either you will or you won't.
It is harder to be unjust towards oneself than towards others.

CONTENTMENT

Zeola Redding

And be content with such things as ye have.
Hebrew 13:5

Be careful what you ask for, you might get it.
The grass is not always greener on the other side.
Everything that glitters ain't gold.
Don't jump out of the skillet into the fire.
Don't bite off more than you can chew.
Everything that looks good to you ain't good for you.
Don't worry about what you can't fix.
Don't overcook the grits.
Don't let any grass grow under your feet.

COOPERATION

Willie Mae Alexander

Can two work together except they be agreed?
Amos 3:3

Too many spoons in the pot spoil the meal.
A horse and a mule can't pull the same wagon.
You can get more with honey than vinegar.
One monkey don't stop the show.
Take a rock off the wagon makes it easier to pull.
Two heads are better than one.
It takes two to tango.
You can take a horse to the water but you can't make him drink.
Oil and water don't mix.
Don't always rock the boat.

FINANCE

Marguerite Watt

*Dishonest money dwindles away,
but he who gathers money little by little makes it grow.
Proverb 13:11*

An even swap is no swindle.
Nothing from nothing leaves nothing.
Naught from naught leaves naught.
A bird in the hand is worth two in the bush.
Don't rob Peter to pay Paul.
Too poor to buy a gnat a wrestling jacket.
A fool and his money will soon depart.
It's a poor rat that ain't got but one hole.
There is no such thing as a free lunch.
Don't count your chickens before they hatch.
Why buy the cow when the milk is so cheap?
A penny earned is a penny saved.
Penny wise, pound foolish.
Fair exchange sho ain't no robbery.
If you give a dance you gotta pay the band.
You don't have a pot to piss in or a window to throw it out of.
Some days you can't borrow a dime.
You pays your nickel and you takes your chance.

PARENTING

Earline Henry

Hear my son and receive my sayings,
and the years of your life will be many.
Proverb 4:10

The apple don't fall too far from the tree.
A tree can only bend when it's a twig.
If you want to make an omelet, you got to crack a few eggs.
The tail shouldn't way the dog.
Don't get to big for your britches.
What a child says, he has heard at home.
Children of the same mother do not always agree.
Home affairs are not talked about in public.
Children should be seen and not heard.
I brought you in this world and I can take you out.
Mama is always right.
'Cause I said so.
A hard head makes a soft behind.
Don't 'spute my word.

PERSEVERANCE

Precious Calloway

Therfore take up the whole armor of God that you may be able to withstand in the evil days and having done all, to stand.
Ephesians 6:13

You have to play the hand that's dealt to you.
Charcoal doesn't get hot until it turns gray.
If you can't stand the heat, get out of the kitchen.
If you can't play with the big dogs, stay out of the yard.
Learn to roll with the punches
When things go wrong, don't go wrong with them.
The sun doesn't shine on the same dog's back all of the time.
The wind does not break a tree that can bend.
Just be still.
You must eat the elephant one bite at a time.
Anyone who says they never had a chance, never took a chance.
The mess you created is the one you must get out of.
You make your bed hard; you have to lay in it.
If it ain't one thing, it is another.
You can't run with the sun and the moon.
You can't burn all day and glow all night; even a light bulb has to be turned
    off sometimes.
It's an ill wind that don't never change.
You got to take the bitter with the sweet.
Never bite off more than you can chew.
You have to take the bull by the horns.
Live until you die.
If you are not going to make the trip, don't get on the train.
Pee or get off the pot.
The darkest hour is just before dawn.

RELATIONSHIPS

John and Eva Butler

***If it be possible,
as much as lieth in you, live peaceably with all men.
Romans 12:13***

You don't miss your water until the well runs dry.
Don't let what others eat make you sick.
If you lay down with dogs you will get fleas.
Not everyone has to have a front row seat in your life.
Even water seeks its own level.
Relationships are like bus rides:
if they are going in the wrong directions you can pull the cord and get off.
Don't change horses in the middle of the stream.
Beware of the dog that brings you a bone.
The person that travels alone has no problems
Love many, trust few, and always paddle your own canoe.
Money can't buy love.
Same things that make you laugh, makes you cry.
What you do to get them, you have to do to keep them.
Same thing men do for you, they will do against you.
If you put a snake to your bosom, don't be surprised when it bites you.
Let the shovel go with the shit.
The more you stir shit, the more it stinks.
The hunter sometimes gets caught by the game.
Sweep around your own front door before you sweep around another.
There's a thin line between love and hate.
You can't teach an old dog new tricks.
It's a poor dog that doesn't piss around his tree.
If the dog bites you the first time it is the dog's fault;
if it bites you a second time, it is your fault.
You can take a horse to the water but you can't make him drink.
Kill 'em with kindness.
A person used to a donkey doesn't ride a horse.
Blood is thicker than water.
It is better to have loved and lost than never to have loved at all.
Two is a couple, three is a crowd.
If you go looking for trouble, you'll find it.
Don't confuse love with loving.
Desperate people do desperate things.

Don't take no wooden nickels.
Nothing can be loved or hated unless it is first known.
You never know who will bring you the last glass of water.
Don't mind your neighbor's fence before looking at your own.
Absence makes the heart grow fonder.
The best way to get even is to forget.
Where you lay your hat is your home.
What goes around comes around.
It takes two to tango.
What one hopes for is always better than what one has.
One reason a dog has so many friends: he wags his tail instead of his tongue.
There's more than one way to skin a cat.
Let every tub sit on its own bottom.
You can't make chicken salad out of chicken shit.
Every dog has its day and a good dog has two.
Don't rain on my parade.
What you eat won't make me fat.
If you always do what you have always done, you will always get what you
    always got.
When the cat is away, the mice will play.
A rooster does not sing on two roofs.
You can't suck and blow at the same time.
An egg can't fight with a rock.
A rat is not afraid in the presence of a dead cat.
A turtle know where to bite another turtle.
You don't have a dog in the fight or a nickel in that dime.
A rolling stone gathers no moss.
Don't piss in my face and call it rain.
Give 'em enough rope to hang themselves.
You can't chase two rabbits at the same time; you'll end up catching nothing.
The chase is better than the catch.
What's done in the dark will come to the light.
Beware of the snake in the grass.
Everybody talking about heaven ain't going there.
Out of sight, out of mind.

SUCCESS

Florence Pendleton

I can do all things through Christ which strengthened me.
Phillippians 4:13

Success comes in cans, failures comes in can'ts,
If you don't toot your horn, nobody else will.
You can't get blood from a turnip.
Doing well is the best revenge.
He, who laughs last, laughs best.
Even a blind dog will find a bone every now and then.
Anything beats a blank.
Sun doesn't shine on nobody's butt all the time.
More the monkey climbs the tree; the more of his behind you see.
It's a poor frog that doesn't praise his own pond.
Everybody loves a winner.
It is better to aim at something and miss than to aim at nothing at all.
Nothing fails without a try.
Nothing beats failure but a try.

TIME AND TIMING

Lavonia Butler

Let us not be weary in well doing;
for in due seasons we shall reap, if we faint not.
Galatians 6:9

There is a time and a place for everything.
There's always tomorrow.
Things that are not eternal are always out of date.
You got to crawl before you can walk.
They saw you coming.
You got to know when to hold 'em and when to fold 'em.
A stitch in time saves nine.
Time waits on no man.
Haste makes waste.
Never change a winning hand, change a losing one.
When you are angry count to ten; if you are still angry count to 100
One day at a time.
Every goodbye ain't gone.
Everything must come to an end.
It's not over until it's over.
Better late than never.
Time heals all wounds.
Strike while the iron is hot.
Shit happens.

WISDOM

Iola Garrett

He who restrains his words has knowledge,
and he who has a cool spirit is a man of understanding.
Proverb 17:27

Never buy a pig in a bag.
Feed some people with a long handle spoon.
Every good yes deserves a good no.
Ain't no fool like an old fool.
Walk softly but carry a big stick.
Even the wind has ears.
Don't let the right hand know what the left hand is doing.
Don't be the same fool twice.
Don't bite the hand that feeds you.
Play your cards close to your chest.
Loose lips sink ships.
Everybody's business is nobody's business.
A lie don't care who tells it.
Don't let your lips overload your behind.
It ain't so much in hearing as in understanding.
There is more wisdom in listening than in speaking.
You don't need a weatherman to tell you which way the wind is blowing.
Got to learn to read between the lines.
Nobody tells all he knows.
Seeing is better than hearing.
Seeing is better than believing.
One must talk little and listen much.
Let a sleeping dog lay.
Don't say the first thing that comes into your mind.
The secret to being a bore is to tell everything.
A hint to the wise is sufficient.
Life will offer you either lessons or blessings.
Never put a period where a comma ought to be.
If it ain't broke, don't fix it.
Easy comes, easy goes.
Talk is cheap.
A new broom sweeps clean.
If you dig one hole, dig two. The first one is for you.
I the shoe fits, wear it.

You can't saw sawdust.
Sometimes a wolf wears sheep clothing.
Lightning don't strike in the same place twice.
If you continue to take the same pitcher to the well, it will eventually break.
No sense in closing the gate once the chicken gets out.
Squeaky wheels get the oil or sometimes get replaced.
Every closed eye ain't sleep.
Don't put the cart before the horse.
Don't pee upwind.
A goat never grazes in the same place.
Don't throw away the baby with the bath water.
Don't throw away the oars before the boat reaches the shore.
You can not teach the old gorilla a new road.
You can grow older without growing old.
Be swift to hear, slow to speak.
A day without laughter is a day without sunshine.
Men are born equal, but they are also born different.
A man is richest whose pleasures are the cheapest.
Faith moves mountains.
In charity there is no excuse.
Where there is smoke, there is fire.
The same man never steps in the same river twice.
Misery loves company.
If it don't fit, don't force it.
Where there is a will, there is a way.
You can not hide the smoke of the house you set on fire.
Don't let your eyes be bigger than your stomach.
Even the night has eyes.
If you climb up the tree you must climb down the same tree.
If the bull frog had wings he wouldn't bump his hind parts so much.
You don't need new shoes to cut a rug.
You have two ears and one mouth to listen twice as much as you talk.
Let the shove go with the shit.

WORK

Carrie L. Tolliver

For as the body without the spirit is dead,
so faith without work is dead also.
James 2:26

Anything worth doing is worth doing right.
An idle mind is the devil's workshop.
The prayers of the chicken hawk don't get him the chicken.
Much effort, much prosperity.
Success is simply a matter of luck. Ask any failure.
Need mo' is the mother of invention.
The rooster crows, but the hen delivers.
What comes with ease goes with ease.
Chance favors prepared minds.
It's your little red wagon, so you got to pull it.
The world is full of willing people; some willing to, and the rest willing to
    let them.
Better to do something than nothing.
Don't put off till tomorrow what can be done today.
Don't wait 'til it is raining to buy an umbrella.